One Thousand Plastic Trinkets

Nick Armbrister

Copyright© 2020 Nick Armbrister
ISBN: 978-81-948271-9-1

First Edition: 2020
Rs. 200/-

Cyberwit.net
HIG 45 Kaushambi Kunj, Kalindipuram
Allahabad - 211011 (U.P.) India
http://www.cyberwit.net
Tel: +(91) 9415091004 +(91) (532) 2552257
E-mail: info@cyberwit.net

No part of this book may be reproduced or transmitted in any form or by any means, electronic, mechanical, photocopying, or otherwise, without the express written consent of Nick Armbrister.

Printed at Repro India Limited.

Dedication

This book is dedicated to aeroplanes everywhere.

Nick loves you all.

Contents

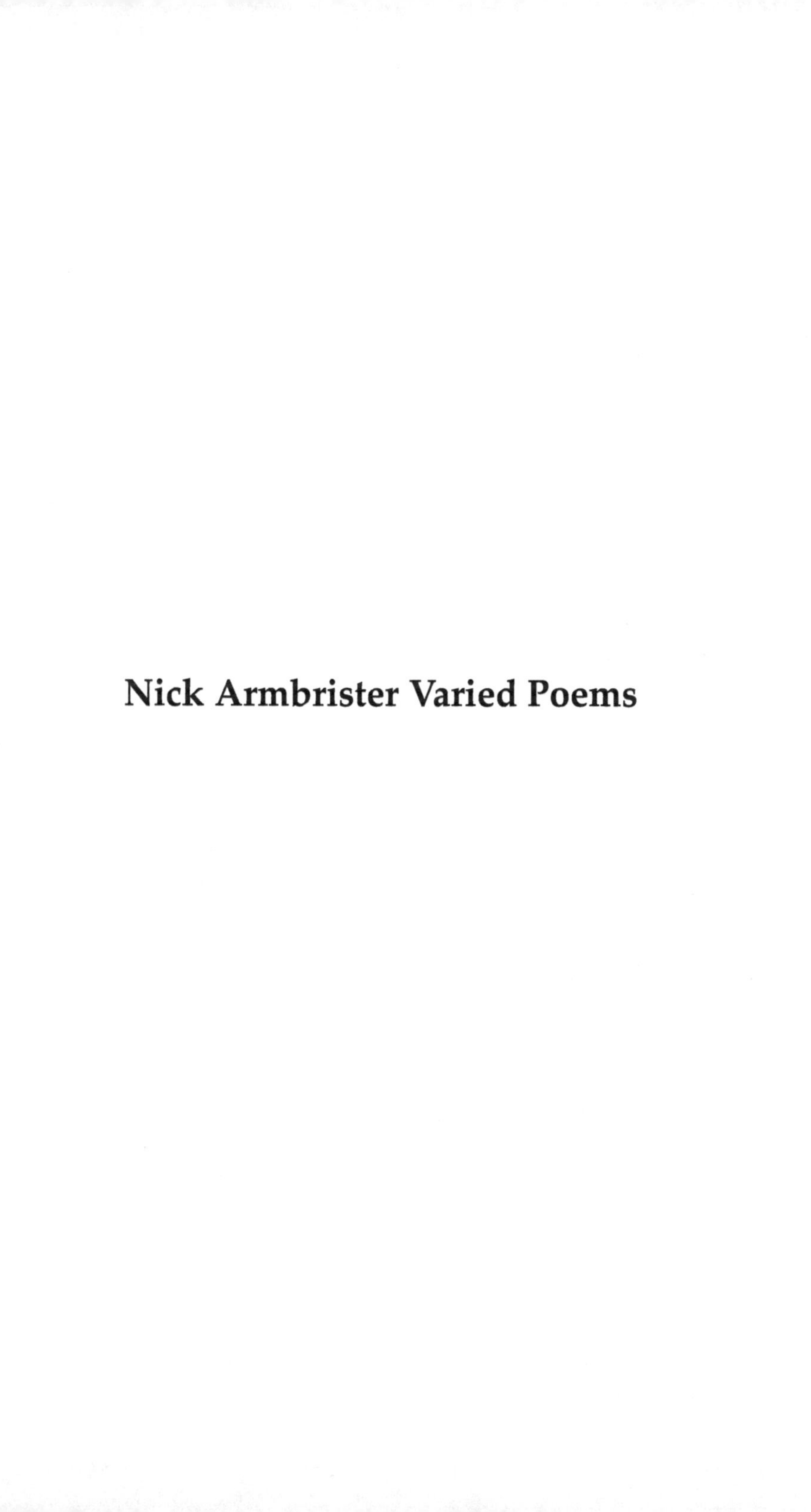

Nick Armbrister Varied Poems

mount gideon

future wars will
be parity battle
cursed even scales
- no winner only
losers and dead
and coffin makers

Normalacyisation

Imagine a normal person who was just that
All things ordinary so as not to shock people
Doing the boring things in life to be in the middle
Adult Orientated Rock not to freak the thought cops out
And reading simple Reader's Digest books
It was like this for the basic man called Stephen

He washed his car every Sunday and took his wife shopping
His wife was the same just like him very much the… same
To see them together you'd look past them unnoticed
What would happen if you put this normal guy
Far away on another planet full of other people
These other people would totally fear him

Immediately hate him for the unknown and obvious
His boring look and boring dress style was subliminal
Sending messages real or not to this alien populace
Threatening everything that they knew and held dear
A crack in their perfect horizon of their beautiful world
A world which we would think wacky odd crazy and weird

Not the same weirdness they think of Stephen who is normal
On this alien world far from Earth he is the threat
A threat to a population that lives within strict boundaries
Anything outside them is hearsay witchcraft alien and the Devil
Now poor normal man was very much noticed which he hated
He wanted to be one of the grey people blending into the background
Not a threat to anyone or anything never mind feared and
misunderstood

This is how is was for poor Stephen stranded on a foreign world
How he wished he was washing his car and walking his dog
Would he become dictator of this world or a victim of it?

In Size

How long ago is yesterday?
It might as well be long
So long that you forget
And become the cliché of you
Younger than forever

But older than time
How long is long enough?
You forget what you ate
Yet remember star birth
Why is that?

Aren't all important
The grand scheme failed
Or did it when it made you
What if you made it?

I Loved The Girl Who Died

In my dream I met her thru her beautiful writing
I guess you could say I loved her due to her extraordinary poems
I wanted to do a book with her
Half hers' half my poems a work of art
But it's not possible for dear Claire is dead

She died two years ago in a car crash

Nothing could be done now except the book
This lady will live on in her words
I met her sister at the village
Much happened that day enough for ten books and a film

I want to tell you all of it

How I went there to demolish the village
A new runway was to be built
All had to move after being paid off
Claire's house was the last one
She wrote all her one off poems there

Her sister gave me all of her poems

Nine thousand of them
She gave me the house and deeds
We had our drink in the local pub
She became my friend and wife

It should've been Claire

I stopped the runway from being built
Now Claire's sis is pregnant
I've no 'job' as I was immediately fired
I stood up to my old boss in court
It was a decade but we won the lawsuit

Claire's village was saved from being a runway

They built it fifty miles away
I never knew that this would be
I love both Claire and her sister Rosa
Claire once did a poem about a man
She sounded so happy
I'm sad that Claire died

But I gained so much more…

One of Those Girls

How many *times* have we been here Nick?
Wondering about the gals that got *away*
The *lovely* 18 year old when I WAS 16
Who wanted me but I said a Mother *joke*
Right thru to HMH now Luna who said *No*!
You only think of *that* yet how we conversed
And a host of *others* where we flew away
And many many more *superb* ladies
Mixed in with a host of *mongers* hahaha
Did I do ok or great or in the middle?
So easy to say in the middle *MOR*
How easy is it to say America 04 with HMH
Or a *great* English what if July 26 1987 with who?
I was oh so shhh *quiet* back then
I *think* of the gal age 14 who had
3 16 year olds *not* me or my mate!
And *what* of the 14 year old lad and his gal
I caught them *party* fucking on my dad's bed
In time I caught up and *surpassed* them all
There were *ones* before and after
I once kept a *list* of the females
Who I fucked or made love to
Full fucking orgasmic penetration!
I *destroyed* it and cast it out out out
Now they live on in my *art*
Were *you* one of those girls hehe?

Painter

When it comes to art
There is no sacrifice
Not worth it.
You see,
It's mesmerizing.
The beauty and cost...

IR

Those five years of 1987 and 1991
When there was nobody and no one for me
Except myself kingdom of me
Things happened all the wrong ways
Dealt with it myself and it showed
I did survive and now look back
If only I had known how it would be...

ol' tom

there was a 20 year old man
who married a 75 year old woman
he said he loved her
but we thought he was mad
totally fucking crazy
fruit loop style
we could understand
if she was a rich heiress
or an ex play boy model
but she was just a pensioner
with nothing but her memories
of a past life now gone
while he was a young buck stood
maybe it was love
mixed with madness…

Photos

The memorials showed the photos of each soldier killed
Cut down by enemy fire be it bullets or rockets
Two hundred dead in Poltava
Five hundred and fifty from Dnipro

Adding to the ten thousand plus dead
Made up of military and civilian lives
Each one forever a life taken
Each a unique story

A unique death
Big brother Russia turned on Ukraine
Putin took his time plotting and planning
His choice was an almost easy kill…
…or was it?

Dancing with Joan Jett

Dancing close with Joan Jett is so wild, it's 1988 and we go head to head. I'm the teen kid by the juke box and she is my wet dream in black leather, one foot in front of me. Pure bloody ecstasy. Garage music blares out of the speakers and we spin around, my arm catching her waist. Closer we draw; a kiss. First of many.

Joan and Nick. Who would have thought it? Rock n roll music heroine meets a Lancashire lad in an intimate spit and sawdust gig venue in a nameless town. It happened, was happening now. 25 July 1989. A day before I was eighteen.

By chance I got her gig ticket, last minute rush. Left my crap job and mental northern town and took the train to see Her, Joan Jett. My teen rock goddess singing live. How many guys wanted a piece of her? And a few gals too. Black leather, boots and an awfully short skirt...

Age 16...

U for Underwear. I dreamt of you in your underwear. You looked very alluring and I wanted you. You tickled my fancy and the rest is history. Full of clichés just like you. So sexy in your underwear. I imagine how you'll look out of it. I'll peel it off you so you're naked. Then I'll kiss you all over especially between your legs. Oh what joy when you cum over my face! Then we'll make love and cum together. My seed in you. Us doing unbelievable things. But then I woke up alone with a huge hard on! And where were you my underwear girl? It was just a reverie.

Two Millimetres (dedicated to the world's chefs and associated staff)

It takes a special person to work in a restaurant's kitchen.
A narcissist.
Not just being able to cook or having a passion for food.
Some learn it, the best are born with it.
Head Chef, is it lonely at the top?
Join your team and drink wine.

Even the dishwasher is important.
You make culinary cuisine a science.
Forks spaced two millimetres apart, measured by ruler.
Your white restaurant is so minimalist.
Like a rocket design laboratory.
What do you go through to get that top award?
Used, abused, make the fucking food!

If it's not perfect you must throw it away.
Fish scallops exactly two millimetres thick.
Yet so many people starve on London's streets.
The art you create s gone in thirty years
unless caught in a picture book.

Why must you be such a bad arse,
always swearing and being bossy?
Who bosses you about?
Your rival hates you but needs you.
As you do him.

He says you are the best.
The Head Chef is like God.
Is that a role you want?
Chef, you exist in a world where you have to trust.
They're your family.
You can't do it alone.

Happily Down

Alba Girl swam with her mermaid friend
They were fifty metres down on the soft sand
The sea bed sloped gently downwards
Little sunlight came this far down
But it was fine for Alba Girl had good eyes
Other senses helped her navigate
She could dive down miles but was fine here
Alba Girl arced round and chased her pal
The mermaid was a good fast swimmer
Giving the dead lady a real competition
It was no contest for Alba Girl drew level
And easily went past her friend
Who responded with a grin and roll
Playfully making bubbles with her tail
And kicking up fine sand off the bottom
Alba Girl found a nice red sea shell
And gave it to her friend as a gift
The mermaid replied with a long kiss
They were more than dear friends

dear regret

hahaha hollow laff/does anyone have more/more regrets than me?/mine is a long list/so many of life's regrets/its fine regrets are cool/what could've been/do you want to add?/be my next sweet or savage regret/like the darling yankee gal/or those illigit kids/or failed jobs/or golden air force career/i'm just a regret collector/now memoried in words/like you my dear regret

More Wanted

How many people have it all and want more?
Just one more toffee from the box
Or one more lady to make love to
Or a car 10 miles per hour faster
Is the grass always greener?
Step over the fence to see
There's no way back over tho
Make a choice and away you go
Cross your fingers it's better
Are all people like this?
May I look inside their heads?
Then I'll know all the answers
I'll stay here at least for now
I'll observe the winners and losers

Strangers, we fuck/hot strong sweet milky cof-
fee/we fuck strangers

Grab

Bored within I see what tomorrow will bring,
today I need more. To replace the bad bits
and have it okay we shall see what life brings,
now to this place that's mine.
A new flat, a job, maybe a girl, no more trauma
for me anymore. These are my needs—
can I attain them in this money-grabbing world?

Clipped

Night crawler is gonna get you.
Do unsaid unholy things to you.
Steal your crucifix and then some.
Ask your God for help.
He'll send down the Devil.
Or send up?

Then the party begins.
Two degenerate demons fighting over you.
Aren't you popular?
Life and soul of the party.
Both soon to be stolen.
Will you try to plead for your
life or take it like a man?
Depending on what they do to you.

Maybe they'll take away your good looks.
Snip off your balls.
Stitch up your mouth.
Turn you into a tree.
All at fucking once.

Night crawler you become.
Deviant of the forgotten time.
Loved by none, feared by all, known to two.
God and the Devil.
Enjoy the ride.

Big Rig Driver

The truck driver loved his wife more than he loved his truck
His big rig was his pride and joy just like his wife
He also loved fucking hookers that were at truck stops
In his career he'd fucked thousands of diverse ones
And driven dozens of different big rigs
Carrying all types of loads from oil to lumber
But the only love of his life was his wife
No matter how powerful or cool his truck
Nor how good the drunken climax
Or how many times he endured both
It was always for her, his wife of thirty six years
This was why he drove coast to coast
And north to south earning his pay
To feel his one true love, his punk rocker wife
The big truck and whores were part of the job
Of the long distance trucker who kept America functioning
And who in turn had wives who kept them going

Before She Fades (On a dream who are you girl?)

I see you you've come back to see me
You all in black trouser suit
With a bit if lipstick not needed

You're slim and medium height with tied back hair
We get on well you tell me how you feel

I say I've done a poem for you
I fumble in my book to find it
So many messy pieces here

Where is it?

I was just working on the bit where we need sex
Yet me being tired got in the way
You tell me things and do so now
That you are horny and want me

I know your long workday will vanish
What we should do now is screw hard like strangers
For we still are arnt we?

Me the mess, the messy writer, you the normal gal
I see you before me as I did the last 3 Saturdays
We will go now to be together
I am grateful you are here

Please know that and I do love you

I who can't even organize my poem book
I need a new journal I'll steal one from work
Come my dear you look lovely in my dream
Whisper me your name dream lady

I love you please don't vanish

I know you're real in my dream and head
But different here in my words
For I forget things but not how I feel
I'm sorry you've been hurt before

I like it when you smile...

Monday

Quick! Arm the army
Lucifer has gone barmy
Where's the witch when we need her?
Having a strop, the silly mare
Stoke the anger of battle
This is more than tittle tattle
Rumours be damned

Satan's got this thing planned
She primed up her flying disc
A big win came with equal risk
With luck her enemy would be drunk
His power, penis and ego may have shrunk
Like the niceness he once had
Before he went all black and bad

Getting the boot from God upon high
So much became nigh!
It was up to the witch now
To turn the Devil into a cow!
With cunning and luck
She'll hit him like a damn truck

And end this thing
Like a failed bloody fling
But that was impossible
Like a flying pig was possible

Soldier Types

What type of man becomes a soldier?
All types of man from a baker to accountant
From the criminal offered either jail or the army

To the graduate who wanted to become a man
All signed up and were given a number
Along with a rifle and uniform and orders
Off to war they went aged 18-22

Keen to show they were ready and able
To kick both German and Japan where it hurt
This they did hundreds of times over

But after Germany and Japan kicked them
Killing their buddies and losing them battles
After these harsh lessons America stood up
Making a stand to do what was needed

Smash the Axis militaries two front war
First Imperial Japan and then Nazi Germany
But it was soon apparent that both were equal

One threat the same as the other
But different in their make up
Yet the same in their fighting intent to win
Both were heavy weight opponents

With skill and tenacity and a knockout will
This was the nature of the enemy to fight
The Army of Democracy stood up

And took on the challenge to be victorious
Once and for all even if it took forever
And cost every single soldier his young life
They started the war we'd finish it

Pretense To Pretend

You pretend that you can fly
Open the window so high
And take a step outwards
What will happen afterwards?
When you've fallen to your death
You took your last breath
But we are getting far ahead
Your thin arms are spread
Now you are in the air
If you fall is that fair?
A million people gasp
You ascend beyond grasp
Proving it can be done
No risk but what fun!
You roll loop and dive
How does it feel to be alive?
Into the blue like an eagle
In no way illegal
Making idiots believe
No lies will they weave
For all have seen
What should be unseen
A human fly above them
Perfect visual gem!

ECHO GIRL

My girl and me ventured into deepest intergalactic space in our Echo Class space ship to see the stars zooming past distant suns and out flying a black hole, a routine trip for me and my lady. One time I'd never of thought it possible that HMH would be by my side but then I never knew that out precious Planet Earth would be burnt to a cinder by the sun. Now we are together we loop through our new solar system near where our new planet is, a virgin world just for us where we can start again and be a family populating this new world. We both asked the pilots who flew an Echo Class if we could both be space pilots and to our surprise they agreed; now we have our own ship to do our own little surveys of our new solar system. It's not like our old one but hey this is home, I've got HMH and she has me and we have our planet and a ship to call our own. Will we soon be joined by another?

DEATH

"My special child, you will soon be with your soulmate. Yes, your soul is empty, torn in two. Your dead love is the same; don't fret, as you will soon be together. Now you must find a way to be there: journey to a place where your end can be symbolic, in a place you will be together with him.

"There is no pain like loneliness and no heaven like being together with your lost love, permanently. Soon it will be so, so don't worry, my young one.

"Go to the lake, to the frozen lake of death. There you will die…"

Office Politix

They do all manner of things in the call centre
Like fucking one another in the boss' office
Right on his big mahogany desk
When he's on holiday leave
They also use his chair

Leaving stains that could only be one thing
But that's ok as you don't care
Getting known or caught is part of it

You face the CCTV as you strip naked
Wobbling your nice pert tits
And fingering your hairy pussy
Knowing it's all recorded

You and your pal are a right pair
Never getting fired or punished
Not even when you both fuck
In five different positions

Is this because the CCTV tape does the rounds?
You both spice things up in the firm
BPO work is so dull so a pick-me-up is needed

Rumour has it that you soon start a list
Offer a prize of who gets to fuck you
Right on CCTV in the boss' office
I want a chance…

Thailand

Six people shared an online post on Facebook
They weren't the creator of the post
But agreed with the contents so shared it
A week later each got a threatening letter
It was off a solicitor company and for libel

Telling the people to contact the firm
Or face the consequences for libel
And also defamation of character
Oddly the letter named the solicitor firm
Acting for the client whose name was withheld

Each of the people never knew who it was
Unless they remembered the name
From the online post they shared
A certain politician who wanted to cover his butt
And not be slandered or libeled or called names

It was he who contacted the firm of briefs
To get them to send out six different letters
And withheld his name to the post sharers
He also worked with the police and detectives
Two related but separate law enforcements

One of the people found out a full check
Was made against themselves for terrorism
Shouldn't all have been checked out?
And what of the slippery politician?
Does he hide behind the law or abuse it?
Have a think about that

Devil Fingers

Red China has gifted our world with ten bad things
What will the next ten bad things be?
Worse or better than the current ten
I think it'll be something different
Yet we'll be familiar with it
And think we can cope but won't
Ten new special gifts from the CCP
All turtles to a corrupt party member
But shh they are all equal no greed there
Rebranding capitalism in their own evil needs
Selling more phones and TVs for new jets and bombs

First Song

It's all rock n roll n goth n metal
Being played from the decks
Oh turn it up loud it's my song!
That track got me into real music
Time stands still when I hear it
Just like yesterday when it was out
Played on the radio and in pubs
In clubs too when only bands mattered
Soundtrack to my early life
Those were the days and I think
They never ever went away
I still listen when I can to it
That special song that I own it
For I dedicated my life to it
And still do decades later
There will never be a song
On the same level or as good
At least not to me

The Mech

The CCP virus killed a million
And infected millions more
Then collapsed economies
In one location a Mechanism was in place
An important question was asked
What happens when the CCP Virus gets too much?
With the 2nd and 3rd and 4th outbreaks

Will the Mechanism be unleashed by the Boss?
His Mechanism set up for his Drug War
Conveniently turned onto the Commies
And Muslim Terrorist Extremists
And used on any and all opponents
It doesn't matter if a few innocent die

Will the CCP Virus Infected by hit next?
The infected people are next
The Mechanism being used to 'reduce numbers'
Thus allowing the medical system to relax
We will see if the Mech is used
And three million infected die…

THROUGH MY EYES

I have seen many things through my eyes.
I see magic, mystical places, angels and fighter planes.
I see the magic of a summers day high in the mountains.
I see surreal dreamers flying through the rarefied air.
I see Gothic maidens dressed in long black dresses
dancing under the moon.
I see a Spitfire turning on a knife-edge,
sun reflecting off its wing.
I see Julianne singing crystal songs that shatter
the twilight dawn.
I see a quartz crystal cast a halo of colours.
I see the beauty of the written word through poetry.
I see the heartbeat that is the life of the moon and of
planet earth and I see the beauty of love and the
violence of war.

BACK O' PUB

We went into the pub's beer garden to see the illegal vodka
factory run by Eastern Europeans.
We dance madly around their lorry and sing, "Give us a drink!
We're parched like the Gobi Desert. Don't you know? We drank
the pub dry? Vodka time."
The Easties open the wagon side curtains and give out the booze.
A one litre bottle each.
We get it on and thank the Albanian and Hungarian gangster
illegal immigrants for their Xylene flavoured vodka.
It's New Years Eve and we get it on big time.
Excuse me while I pop into the truck's cab with my exotic lady
and make love. Then we need more vodka.
Shame the bar is dry.
Oh my, we're so drunk...

25cc Moped

The 25cc moped was so very cool
It had a two stroke 25cc engine
A full body fairing with space
Under the seat for the rider's helmet
Was fitted with bright LED lights
And a neon digital display for the speed
Not to mention a comfy green double seat
The off road tires were big and chunky
And the body was painted blue
All in all this moped was cool
Even if illegal on most roads
The engine was just too small
But it was fine for the sticker said:
125cc and nobody questioned the lie
Allowing me to ride my moped
Wherever I wanted
At a top speed of 30mph
To whizz on by

1989 Girl All is Fine

All I wanted was to be loved
Do you not see that?
30 years ago I was 17

I wanted my alternative goth girl
The one in the purple skirt
I wanted her to call to the house

And say she missed me and loved me
That it would be all ok Nick
And nobody will hurt you

With words or fists or threats
But you never did walk up to my path
Never knocked on my door

Or walked thru my door
You never even existed
Except as an idea or dream

I am sorry
Why?
You never existed

Written Or Spoken

We write for the reason of writing. Name it more or less than that. The simple reason of writing. To write. Whether it's a shopping list or an epic novel. Words down on paper. Simple and important.

Words said to a hit man. On who to rub out. An amount of cash agreed. A deed done. A boss who doesn't listen. Sending the company into the red. Time to leave before court case and jail.

Whispered incantations to a Goddess or God of your choice. For love or hate. Your choice. Did you get what you wanted? Or do only you and your deity know? Aliens communicating in images equal words.

Wireless commands through the ether. Picked up by spies, allies and enemies alike. Numbers on the radio. Voice mails to yourself. Are you mad? No, you've no friends and enjoy your own voice.

Wave understood. Bike gang changes formation and forms up. Ready to attack. Graphic health warning for rednecks. Hunting rifles versus machine pistols. Who will win? Only words. Spoken or written.

Darts

Isn't is so awesomely amazing that a paper dart type plane and the legendary Aurora spy plane (which is dart like from the fan art) look almost the same.

One flies a couple of miles per hours and a few feet and the other at mach 6 and thousands of miles.

If the Aurora exists, imagine they designed it based upon a paper dart plane.

And designed it while drunk in a bar.

Hcy, this is a good plane design. See how it flies...

Becoming

The machines of metal
Pulp human flesh
They are good at it
And hugely enjoy it

May Song

Maybe one day it will all be alright
Maybe one day I'll figure life out
Maybe one day I'll understand myself
Maybe one day life will give me its answers
Maybe one day I'll ask the right questions
Maybe one day I'll find out the reason why
Maybe one day all will be a dream
Maybe one day I'll start it all again
Maybe one day I simply forget what I am
Maybe one day I'll ascend to the stars
Maybe one day I'll be a computer program
With no feelings or fucking issues

From a Story…

I see the flirt girl sat there
Right next to me
I know she wants me
From her body language
And from when she says it:
I feel so horny
I go over the facts
Her body gave birth to four
Tho her figure is still slim
And her legs are great
Going to her ears, almost
Those cut down jeans
Tightly hug her thighs
And her smile lights up
Her face like the sky
Like the moon in the dark
This lady who is a flirt
The worst or best type of girl
Acting half her years
Like she is her own daughter
Half her age 48, 24
Oh what could be if I said yes!
But I don't for I do not want her
In my mind but my body does
If she was fifteen years younger
And had two not four
And understood me
Not misunderstand me
Oh what could be…

Riding her like a bike
Fucking me till dawn
Sucking me dry
And a hundred other things
Never to be
Except in this poem

Turtle Soup

The turtle smokes. So he's a smoking turtle. Loving big fat cherry flavour cigars. I'm in the CCP. Don't ask him who his father is. He'll be very offended. More than if you fucked his sister. Truth told he doesn't know. Poor little turtle. Not knowing who his dad is. And hating being a turtle. Fact denied. You are a turtle. And a bastard. As your father could be anyone. Turtle who's your father? It isn't me. Cos I'm a crazy purple alien who lives in Hitler's cellar. And that's a different story...

Suicide Room

There's a room where people go to do something beautiful and
special.
They go there to commit suicide.
I caught a glimpse of it in a vision after a vodka night when
Emma had forsaken me.
The white wood walls are blood splattered.
Daylight comes thru gaps in a boarded up window by a corner.
A small curved potato peeler knife is what everyone uses.
Such a wicked and effective tool.

People ravaged by despair and failure come here to die.
It's a long list; the knife's always bloody.
Something from that dark multi emotional place came thru my
vision and lodged in me.
What?
A ghost or the reason why?
Why all types of people go there to suicide?
I can't see it; it's hidden.

I do see what 5 years of failure in love has done to me.
Decades can be added to that.
So much shit in my head, life, heart, me.
My turn will soon be here to end my life in that room.
The Suicide Room.

Emma will be next, following me.
Death by razor sharp potato peeler.
Thanx Em.
I started to love you and look what you made me do.

I'm mad at you but don't hate you.
Quite the opposite.
Goodbye.

Life

Life pressures me to have a girlfriend.
Life pressures me to have a day job.
Life pressures me to have a car.
Life pressures me to be mentally stable.
Life pressures me to dress a certain way.
Life pressures me to think a normal thoughts.
Life pressures me to behave in a Politically Correct manner.
I say fuck all this bullshit.
I'm going to be just me.
I'm not a drone like the rest of you sheep.

No Death

Hundreds had died crossing the wall
Paying the ultimate price for freedom
Or imperatively trying to attain it
Did those who made it find happiness?
Was the capitalist West better

Than our totalitarian communist East?

It was home but not our heaven
We did not want to die escaping
Nor did we want to live in jail
We had to be smart

Smarter than them

Their hidden eyes were everywhere
Watching us and missing nothing
We hadn't be caught yet
Being together as one

A forbidden gay couple

Deep in the evil commie empire
This is why we must flee
And be free

Missed Time

I miss my parents greatly
My mum died 5 years ago
And my dad last year
I wish I'd if spent more time
Simply in their presence
Now it's too late
Except in dreams and Halloween
See you on the other side

Blissful Job

I'm off to the factory
Where we listen to Bathory
While making oak coffins
Designed by our mad boffins.

There's a certain cool
In making a box for a fool
A home for the dead
Body cold like lead.

Solid oak has permanence
Unlike life's short temperance
Each breathe a step to death
Ignorant of all one's wealth.

A good job I'm a goth
Unafraid of my own wrath
Doing my humble coffin job
Earning my keep to bury a knob.

Miss

Of lavender skies I dream. Scent of Juniper, summer serenity.
I'm here with you, evermore. No more tomorrow's forsaken.
Here today Cirrus clouds lofty.
I see the hill side; steep, jagged, stunning. Purple rocks, exposed
Earth's soul. Green blood flows thru her. Alive like you, sexy as a
nymph. Her cave is narrow; tight cunt.
Beauty abounds. Let us fly together, ascension. Making love
ethereal empyrean. Unbound of strife and stress. Eternal infinite
love.

My Thing

I decide what I want to do
And then do it especially if fun
Maybe you don't approve
Just keep your views quiet
Until you see how happy I am
Shit happens then and we fight
Till one of us is fucking dead
My war to win no matter what
Eventually I'll carry on with my thing...

Condition

Love is not enough the judge said
I say she is both right and wrong
For love is enough if you do it right
Or love aint enough if you fail
It's all in your head and heart
And depends on your POV
So what do you say?
Is love enough or not?
Myself, I sit on the fence
It depends on my mood
When I'm happy love is enough
Counteracted by my madness to bin it
All part of the human condition

Take The Times

On and on the days of life go and advance
Just like writing a poem or story chapter
We have good and bad days and indifferent
This is the way it is and it goes on and so
Just like water down the plug hole
Days going away till they are years
But what if the water could reverse
And go back up the tap a reversal
You have a bad day well simply relive it
Then it's just another good day
Minimising the crap days and times
The thing is it would be too good
Too much of a good thing till what
Then you wish for dark dreary days!
Sending the good times to the trash
It's a balance of good and bad
But not always possible for some are
Bad suffer negativity and give it away
While others have too much goodness
They get used by the bad people
None of it matters for it's gone
All water down the drain as days go by
On and on the days go like zoo days
We are the star attractions in the show

Potted Sinks

Round around round around on and on and on
Makes me dizzy this crazy fucking thing
That spans decades almost centuries
One time France is the bad guy
Another Germany is the enemy

Then Russia is the opponent

Not to forget Japan pissing many off
And England they were the top one
Now it's Red China who is the bad turtle
In future decades and centuries

New enemies and bad guys will be there

Top of the list wanting to missile you
As you aim your gun at them
Why is it this way the system?
Imagine if it developed differently
Our world would be at peace not war
And the defence complex would be war skint
Making plant pots and kitchen sinks instead

KING FISHER HEART 2

I suppose it's funny, the things that life throws at me, how it all goes to fuck by the slightest mistake!

Am I destined to fail at everything I do, with defeat waiting in the wings to bring my eagle down?

How does one know when a good day crashes down? I know many things but there's always more just waiting to be shown.

I have some scary weird dreams I don't understand – maybe you can help me and make life that bit easier?

You are my king fisher heart ready to fly away – like all I hold dear.

And There Were Three

Late mark Griffon engine Spitfire is sliced apart by German gunfire. Defeat! Spit pilot takes to the silk and bails. He saw his executioner executed. Swift justice handed out by a Tempest. No one said the Salamander was in service.

Volksjager peoples' fighter, for everyone but only flown by the best, killed a Spitfire before a Tempest killed him. Did the Nazi pilot perish? Unlike the Spit pilot? Eyewitness to his own shoot down. Advanced air war 1945, Armageddon beckons.

Enough! Time for a coffee and some biscuits, teen combat pilot dreams aside. I close my book and go to make a brew. No decaf for me. Need my caffeine before I battle the Luftwaffe in turbulent European skies. Shame I've no beer!

Never mind about being there, seeing history made. German jet genesis, almost mastering state of the art piston engine fighters. Back to my book. At 17 my mates were out chasing girls, I was in the skies.

Sopwith Pup

In the cockpit of my biplane
I loop and roll to evade you
You'll never ever beat me
I win each fucking time
I do not need your high tek

No heat seeking missiles
No infra red tracking system
No digital computer systems
No predicative Artificial Intelligence
No advanced do it all radar
No 9 g capable jet fighter
No platform of the 5th generation
No multi million dollar trained pilot
No turn the corner heat seeking rocket
No hundred mile range active radar missile

No all I need is my single seat biplane
It does one hundred miles per hour
Is armed with a machine gun
And I'll blow your fucking head off!

Meeting

What's taking place in the meeting of men?
When they meet in a room or secretly in a forest, things happen.
Ripples leading to the future, untold events like back in 42, Final
Solution style. Millions wiped out due to the racism and hatred of
a madman.

But good can happen too.

Issuing life saving drugs for free, researching a cancer cure,
setting up an animal charity.
Better than deciding to invade a country, build the A-bomb, make
a ballistic missile.
Men can bring positive change.

It starts with an idea.

www.ingramcontent.com/pod-product-compliance
Lightning Source LLC
LaVergne TN
LVHW051508170726
843492LV00002B/849